PREFACE

"To no one will we sell, to no one will we refuse or delay, right or justice." - Magna Carta, 1925.

In absence of enforceability of law, liberty becomes obsolete. Therefore, speedy justice is the foundation of rule of law and it has been a concern for the citizenry, legislature, executive and judiciary. It will be a tragedy if the law is so petrified as to be unable to respond to the unending challenges of evolutionary and revolutionary changes. The Life of the law has not been logic. It has been experience. Any procedure to be efficient and effective has not only to answer the test of logic and principles but also the experience of its actual working in the crucible of investigation, inquiry and trials.

It is a vast subject which knows no limitations or boundaries. I have tried my level best to inculcate universally accepted and adopted judicial trends, so as to make the book a unique combination of law and practice. I hope this book entitled **'Justice Delayed: Bottlenecks & Remedies'** will be very much useful for the legal practitioners, students, academicians and even public in general.

At last, I express a vote of thanks to all concerned and specifically my husband and my family for providing enormous amount of support without which present work was not possible.

(Dr.Ravidankaur R.Karnani)

	TABLE OF CONTENT	Page No.
	Preface	1
	Chapter 1 Mandate of Speedy Justice	
1.	Introduction	5
2.	International Scenerio	8
3.	Ancient Scenerio	9
4.	Judicial Intervention	10
5.	Concept of Delay	12
	Chapter 2 Bottlenecks in Disposal of Old Criminal Cases	
1.	Poor Judge Population Ratio	22
2.	Lack of Sufficient & Efficient Manpower	24
3.	Outdated Infrastructure & Limited Computerization	26
4	Neglect of Old Cases	28
5.	Frequent Adjournment Applications	30
6.	Strikes by Advocates	32
7.	Procedural Bottlenecks	33
	Chapter 3 Doctrine of Trial in Absentia	
1.	Background	44
2.	Origin & Development of Doctrine	47
3.	Trial in Absentia under International Law	50

4.	Nature of Waiver	52
5.	Procedural Safeguards	53
	Chapter 4 Bottlenecks in Disposal of Old Civil Cases	
1.	Non-service of Process	55
2.	Non-framing of Issues	59
3.	Frequent Interlocutory Application	60
4.	Non-Proceeding	62
5.	Case Stayed or R&P Called	63
6.	Approach of Parties	65
7.	Approach of Judges	66
8.	Other Bottlenecks & Discussion	68
	Chapter 5 Judicial Precedents & Guidelines	75
	Chapter 6 Role of a Judge	82
	Chapter 7 ADR & Mediation	87
	BIBLIOGRAPHY	99
	ACRONYMS	

Chapter 1
Mandate of Speedy Justice

"The Life of the law has not been logic. It has been experience. Any procedure to be efficient and effective has not only to answer the test of logic and principles but also the experience of its actual working in the crucible of investigation, inquiry and trials."

Oliver Wendell Holmes, Jr.

In absence of enforceability of law, liberty becomes obsolete.[1] Therefore, speedy justice is the foundation of rule of law and it has been a concern for the citizenry, legislature, executive and judiciary. Quite Often it is said that 'justice delayed is justice denied'. In 1925, Clause 40 of Magna Carta, provided that "To no one will we sell, to no one will we refuse or delay, right or justice."

Speedy justice is a constitutional mandate as well as an essential attribute of the Fundamental Right to Life guaranteed under Art.21. It will be a tragedy if the law is so petrified as to be unable to respond to the unending challenges of evolutionary and revolutionary changes.

---
[1] Wolfgang Friedmann, Law in a changing society, p.503.

But for an average litigant, the court working may not be as smooth as indicated in law books as he is likely to find it to be tedious and cumbersome. At every stage of the trial and appeal, a number of unavoidable and avoidable hurdles come up prolonging cases and indirectly encroaching upon rule of law as a social value. Those who are familiar with judicial procedure would most often manage to prolong the process of the case.

This kind of disturbing situation has not gone unnoticed. The mass media, the academicians and even the superior judiciary have come out with critical observations in respect of those cases which came to light. As a central point of this Book, a small attempt is mades to find out who is really responsible for mounting of arrears. Whether the wheels of Judiciary are slow or the Goverment itself not filling the fuel in the tank.

In Criminal trial, a procedural irregularity is not regarded as fatal, unless it has occasioned in prejudice to the accused in his defense. If there is substantial compliance with the procedure and the accused is not prejudiced and has got a fair opportunity to defend himself, the trial is not vitiated.

But for any procedure to be just, fair and reasonable, it must not undermine the principles on which it stands. The range and Limits of procedural fairness is well settled.[2] by a long line of judicial pronouncements.

The Law Commission in its 77th Report[3] has noted that 'For efficient discharge of the responsibilities of the courts, it is essential that the broad confidence which the people have in the system, the high prestige and the great respect they have enjoyed should be maintained and not be subject to any eclipse. The community has a tremendous stake in the preservation of image of the courts as dispensers of justice. Weakening of the judicial system in the long run has necessarily the effect of undermining the foundations of the democratic structure. Any institution and more so a judicial system is rooted in the society and its success to a large extent depends on the confidence it enjoys of the people who are the principal stakeholders of it.

Erosion of public confidence in it can undermine the foundations of the criminal justice system and may turn people to extra legal means'.

---

[2]Maneka Gandhi v. Union of India, (AIR 1978 SC 597.
[3] Law Commission, 77th Report on delays and arrears in trial court, Para 1.4 Page 77.5 Chapter 1, Public Confidence in Courts.

- **INTERNATIONAL SCENERIO**

Under International Law also, it is well established that every accused must be tried without undue delay. Art. 14(3) of the International Covenant on Civil & Political Rights, 1966[4] specifically mandating the same is reproduced here-

"Article 14. 3. In the determination of any criminal charge against him, everyone shall be entitled to the following minimum guarantees, in full equality:
(a) ....
(b) ....
(c) To be tried without undue delay;
(d) ....
(e) ....
(f) ....
(g) ...."

It is further well settled under the International Law that fairness of trial has to be seen not only from the point of view of the accused, but also from the point of view of the victim and the society. Art. 8 of the Universal Declaration of Human Rights, 1948[5] specifically mandating the same is reproduced here-

"Article 8. Everyone has the right to an effective remedy by the competent national tribunals for acts violating the fundamental rights granted him by the constitution or by law."

---

[4] AccessedOnline-https://treaties.un.org/doc/publication/unts/volume%20999/volume-999-i-14668-english.pdf

[5] Accessed Online-www.un.org/en/udhrbook/pdf/udhr_booklet_en_web.pdf

Therefore, we must learn that all methods are to viewed not as idols but as tools. We must test one of them by the others, supplementing and re-enforcing where there is weakness, so that what is strong and best in each will be at our service in the hour need.[6]

- **Ancient Scenerio**

The imperative need of quick disposal of cases was also felt in ancient times. Its echoes are to be found in Mahabhorat and Ramaycma. In History of Dharamshastra by Dr. P. V. Kane.1973 Ed., Vol. III (page 243) under the head Vyauohora (Law and Administration of Justice), Chapter XI. it is recited : "..... The Mahabharafa (Anusasana 638 and Chapter 70) and Ramayana say that if a King intent on pleasures does not show himself to litigants who approach him for decision, he would suffer like King Nriga. The Sukranitisara (IV 58) also says the same thing. In Ramayana (VIL 53-54) King Nriga is said to have been cursed to become a chameleon for a long period by two Brahmanas who had a dispute about the ownership of a cow and could not see the king for many days. Megasthenes (Frag. XXV1L. pp. 70-71) says "the king remains the whole day in court without allowing the business to be Interrupted".

---

[6] Justice Benjamin N. Cardozo, The Growth of The Law.

Kautilya (1.19) gives the advice that-

"when in court the king should not cause petitioners or litigants to wait long at the door, for when a king makes himself inaccessible, those who are near him create confusion about what should or should not be done, whereby the king engenders disaffection among his subjects and makes himself a prey to hts foes."[7]

- **JUDICIAL INTERVENTION**

Initially, The Supreme Court of India observed that It is neither advisable nor practicable to fix any time limit for trial of offences. Any such rule is bound to be qualified one. Such rule cannot also be evolved merely to shift the burden of proving justification on the shoulders of the prosecution. In every case of complaint of denial of right to speedy trial, it is primarily for the prosecution to justify and explain the delay. At the same time, it is the duty of the Court to weigh all the circumstances of a given case before pronouncing upon the complaint. The Supreme Court of USA too has repeatedly refused to fix any such outer time limit inspite of the Sixth Amendment. Nor do we think that not fixing any such outer limit in effectuates the guarantee of right to speedy trial'.[8]

---

[7] Siddhartha Kumar And Others vs Upper Civil Judge, Senior Division, Para 3, 1998 (1) AWC 593.
[8] Abdul Rehman Antulay v. R.S.Nayak AIR 1992 SC 1701.

In **Raj Deo Sharma v. State of Bihar**[9], the Hon'ble Supreme Court of India attempted to define a time frame for the disposal of criminal cases and it was directed that in cases where the trial is for an offence punishable with imprisonment for a period not exceeding seven years, whether the accused is in jail or not, the Court shall close prosecution evidence
 on completion of a period of two years from the date of recording the plea of the accused on the charges framed whether prosecution has examined all the witnesses or not, within the said period and the Court can proceed to the next step provided by law for the trial of the case and if the offence under trial is punishable with imprisonment for a period exceeding 7 years, whether the accused is in jail or not, the Court shall close prosecution evidence on completion of three years from the date of recording the plea of the accused on the charge framed, whether the prosecution has examined all the witnesses or not within the said period and the Court can proceed to the next step provided by law for the trial of the case, unless for very exceptional reasons to be recorded and in the interest of justice the Court considers it

---

[9] (I) MANU/SC/0640/1998.

necessary to grant further time to the prosecution to adduce evidence beyond the aforesaid time limit.

Though, the above judgement was reversed by the supreme court in the subsequent case, **Raj Deo Sharma v. State of Bihar**[10] and it was held that it is true that ideal situation may be where criminal cases are tried within six months from the date of institution, and appeals are disposed of within a period of one year from the date of filing. For achieving misideal situation, if there is lack of infrastructure and procedural delays for various reasons, then what is required to be done? In such a situation would it be justifiable to acquit the accused after lapse of a particular time if prosecution has failed to examine all witnesses? And, whether the appeal could be dismissed if the appellate authority fails to decide the same within a particular time? To do so, in my view, would not be just and fair for the society and the victims affected by the crimes.'

- **CONCEPT OF DELAY-**

The first and foremost question which arise here is that what should be the criterion to determine as to when a judicial case can be treated as an old case in the trial court?

---
[10] (II) MANU/SC/1655/1999.

In other words, what can be the yardstick to measure when a criminal case can be termed to have suffered delay?

Regarding, the method of computation of delay, the Law Commission of India has opined[11] that 'the time would be calculated from the date of filing of charge sheet or complaint till the date of pronouncement of final judgment. In case of sessions trials, above period should also include the time during which proceedings remained pending before the committing magistrate'. The commission mentioned the average life span of a criminal case to be four to six months.[12]

As per the current practice in Indian courts, the cases pending below 2 years is the ideal life span of a case, below 5 years is the acceptable delay, 5-10 years' life span of a case is considered to be unacceptable delay or the old cases category and for more than 10 years are considered to be the extreme old cases.

---

[11] The Law Commission of India, 77th Report on 'Delays andArrears in Trial courts', para 1.10.
[12] Ibid, para 1.9.

The present state of arrears in our Law Courts and the long delays in the disposal of cases are Justly causing concern. From time to time, public attention has been drawn to this sorry state of affairs and though the matter has been frequently discussed both in the Parliament and outside, yet the problem has defied any solution. A compilation of mostly identical but a few divergent suggestions of eminent jurist. Judges, legislators, committees and commissions would show that all are raising 'alarm' at the mounting arrears and delay in disposal of cases. Almost unanimous view is that unless something 'radical' is done the Judicial system would "crash and collapse under its weight.' There was, no doubt, a time when Judiciary was highly respected by the people who had faith in the quality of justice, dispensed with promptly by the Judges. Now the people have started loosing faith in the entire judicial system because of every day increasing arrears. Remarks have come to be made expressing the lamentation in various forms. The whole nation, it was said, is in a Juridical abyss. Many today are dissatisfied over the courts' conduct. All through the years men have protested at the laws' delay and counted it as a grievous wrong, hard to bear. It is linked amongst the whips and scorns of the time. Some talk of it. how it exhausts patience, courage and hope.

In substance, it is a Judicial anathema, for all who are concerned with the litigation process. Even the aggrieved persons have, at times, been found remorseful and repentant for filing the case. It is a usual phenomenon to hear the conversation between suitors that they are not likely to reap the fruits of litigation during their life time. Eminent Jurists have gone even to the extent of observing that our Justice Delivery System is cracking under the oppressive weight of delay and arrears. It has been repeated ad nauseam that to delay Justice is to deny justice.[13]

Though, the Criminal Procedure Code lays down elaborate stages of investigation, inquiry and trial, since after institution of the F.I.R or filing of the complaint till its conclusion by delivery of judgment by the trial court. The Code normally does not prescribe time limits for different stages. There is no specific time limit for investigation, inquiries or trial, save to a limited extent for sexual offence cases provided by 2013 amendment.

---

[13]Siddhartha Kumar And Others vs Upper Civil Judge, Senior Division, Para 5, 1998 (1) AWC 593.

The frightful problem of mounting arrears of cases in the subordinate courts is one of the greatest challenges which the Judiciary is facing today. It has subjected the Judicial system, as it must, to severe strain. Though the strain at present, is severe, the problem of delay in the disposal of cases is not a recent phenomenon. It has been in existence since a long time. The gradual increase in the institution of cases coupled with failure of disposal to keep pace with them, has resulted in an alarming rise in the pendency of cases in the subordinate courts.

Although time frame has not been laid down in the code for completing the investigation, inquiry or trial, but it cannot be said that the code is completely bereft of any such guideline.

In some cases, the consequences of delay at a particular stage have been provided as default bail[14], maximum detention period for UTP[15], bail option on non-completion of trial[16]

and limitation for cognizance of offences[17].

---

[14] Under section 167 Cr.P.C, which makes provision for statutory bail if the investigation is not completed within the prescribed time frame.

[15] Section 436A Cr.P.C lays down the maximum period for which and under-trial prisoner can be detained during the period of investigation, inquiry or trial under this Code for any offence not punishable with death.

Not only that, the Code of Criminal Procedure further makes it clear that prompt examination of witness is the overriding concern and no routine adjournment can be granted at this stage.[18] Clearly, if the examination of the witnesses is delayed at the stage of trial due to omissions or commissions of the prosecution or defense, the same may be termed as unacceptable delay in violation of the mandate of the Code.

The problem has assumed gigantic proportions inviting scathing criticism. The contributory sources and factors are many. It is not the Judiciary alone which has to hear the bunt of the criticism. To deal with the chronic disease in the body of the administration of justice, several Law Commissions and Committees have scratched their heads to find out a solution to the problem.

---

[16] Under Section 437(6) Cr.P.C if the trial is not concluded within 60 days from the first days of taking evidence and the person accused of the non-bailable offence is in custody throughout the period such person shall be released on bail.

[17] Section 468 Cr.P.C lays down bar to taking of cognizance after the lapse of Six months if the offence is punishable with fine only; One year with the offence is punishable with imprisonment for a term not exceeding one year; Three years, if the offence is punishable with imprisonment for a terms exceeding one year but not exceeding three years.

[18] Section 309 of the Code of Criminal Procedure.

The first Committee, known as Rankin Committee, was appointed in 1924. It was followed by a report of the High Court Arrears Committee, 1949, set up by the Central Government under the Chairmanship of Justice S. R. Das. In 1972, Justice Shah Committee was appointed. The report of Justice Satish Chandra Committee was also submitted and in the year 1990--Malimath report came into being. Besides these reports of the Committees, the Law Commission of India made as many as 14 reports (14th. 22nd. 27th. 54th, 58th. 77th. 79th. 80th, 99th, 120th. 121th, 123rd, 124th and 129th) in one way or the other to deal with the problem of accumulation of huge arrears of cases and disposal of old cases at various stages and levels of courts. The very fact that the problem of arrears has received the attention for such a long time and has been considered by so many high powered Committees, and yet continues to vex all concerned, is enough to indicate that the problem, by its nature, is not so easy to solve. Concern has been voiced by eminent Jurists, administrators, Parliamentarians and politicians at different platforms but the problem still remains unaffected, unabated and unsolved. In the light of the recommendations made by the Law Commission and the various

Committees efforts have been made to tinker with the problem but the surging problem remains insurmountable.[19]

---

[19] Ibid, Para 4.

Chapter 2
Bottlenecks in Disposal of Old Criminal Cases

"To no one will we sell, to no one will we refuse or delay, right or justice."

-Magna Carta[20]

Abuses by King John caused a revolt by nobles who compelled him to execute recognition of rights for both noblemen and ordinary citizen and established the principle that no one, including the king or a lawmaker, is above the law. Therefore, even today, the Magna Carta is recognized as the great charter and the foundation of democratic setups all across the world. But who would have imagined that the largest democratic country of the world would be facing the criticism of 'Justice Delayed is Justice Denied' in 21st Century as mounting arrears of cases eventually results in denying rights of litigants.

Delay in the disposal of criminal cases is a cumulative process. Inordinate delays in the investigation and prosecution of criminal cases is a blot on justice system.

---
[20] Clause 40, Magna Carta (1215).

The objective of penal law and the social interest is thereby frustrated and the fear of law and the faith in the criminal justice system is eroded irretrievably. Delay and huge backlog of cases have become evergreen curse against the Judges. But the government and the bar are equally responsible, if not more than that, for slow wheels of judiciary. The Govt. has not provided sufficient human resource by timely recruiting required number of Judges, public prosecutors and staff members and equipping the judiciary with required I.T. Tools inspite of law commission recommendations, chief Justice meetings references and directions in various judgements.

The bar has also constantly eroded the path of speedy justice by constantly filling adjournment applications and miscellaneous applications even for such triffling issues which can be ordinarily taken care with. The Bar is the better half of the Bench and necessary support is always required on their part for the cause of justice.

However, the blame for huge arrears of old cases is also on the Judges. Yet no system, not even the justice delivery system can be better than the men who man it.

- **Common Bottlenecks in Disposal of Old criminal and civil Cases-**

Under present circumstances, the Hon'ble Chief Justice of India[21] was forced to state that 'my judges are sitting under trees to dispense justice' as there are just 16000 judges to decide 3.2 crore cases & It may take 300 years to clear the backlog. The data also shows that input of cases is higher than the disposal. So by end of every year, the senario will be even worst. Some common bottlenecks responsible for hue backlog of case can be sortlisted as under-

1. Poor Judge Population Ratio-

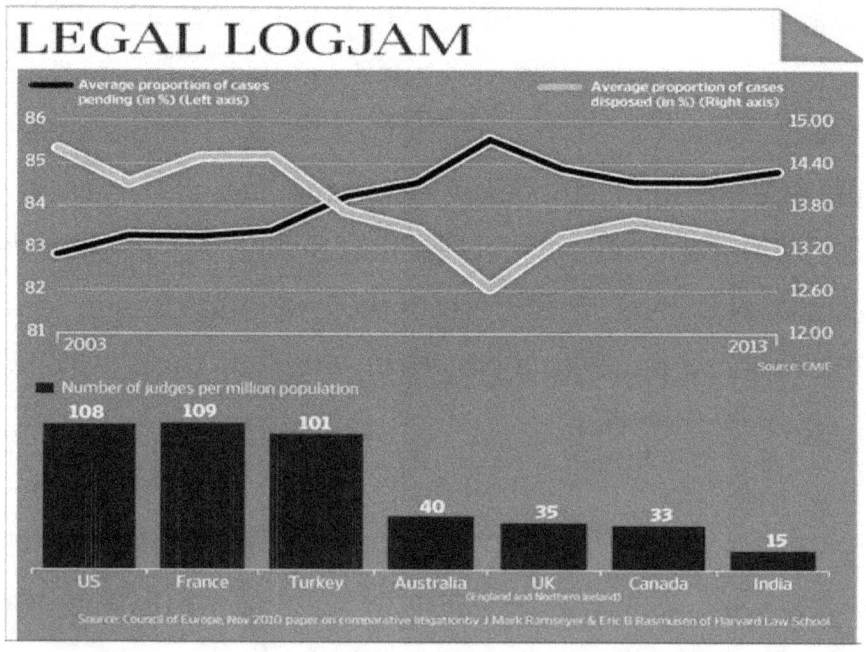

---

[21] Mr. T.S.Thakur in his interview to the Times magzine.

The following chart clearly reflects that a legal logjam has been created by poor judge population ratio in India compared to other developing & developed countries. The Courts do not possess a magic wand by which they can wave to wipe out the huge pendency of cases nor can they afford to ignore the instances of injustices and illegalities only because of the huge arrears of the cases. Lack of sufficient and efficient manpower i.e. Judges, public prosecutors and staff is a considerable aspect of delay in prompt justice.

The Govt. has failed to address this issue but it must now immediately fill the vacant posts at trial court, high court and supreme court level at the first instance and than also creat further posts as per the need of the instituton and must review it tme to time. Equally important is to consider, how much priority govt. is giving to the judiciary in its Budget. As per the information collected by First National Judicial Pay Commission, every state except Delhi has been providing less than 1% of the budget for subordinate judiciary. The following Table presents the true picture of allocation of funds to judiciary compaired with other necessities of life like- education and medical care-

Table- Year-wise % allocation of Budget to Judiciary in Gujarat[22]

S. No.	Year	Judiciary	Social Welfare	Health	Education
1.	2006-07	0.47	6.06	2.74	12.42
2.	2007-08	0.47	7.92	2.66	11.87
3.	2008-09	0.44	9.34	2.67	11.48
4.	2009-10	0.70	9.90	2.91	11.64
5.	2010-11	0.94	2.91	3.63	13.84

The judicial system is set to continue to expand significantly over the next three decades, rising, by the most conservative estimate, to at least about 15 crores of cases requiring at least some 75,000 Courts/Judges. The Governments should not allow their financial constraints to come in the way of increase in the strength of judges. Unfortunately, it hasn't so happened for last many years inspite of many paper promises and commitment on the part of the Government.

2. Lack of Sufficient and Efficient Manpower-

Prosecution in criminal cases is conducted by public prosecutors or govt. pleaders. At present there is big shortage of public prosecutors in criminal courts.

---

[22] SOURCE: NCMS POLICY & ACTION PLAN RELEASED BY: THE SUPREME COURT OF INDIA

At present, an a.p.p. has to handle prosecution in two or three courts or sometimes even more. If the public prosecutors are not available for all working days, recording of evidence will also not possible for all the working days, thereby resulting in less disposal of cases. At least, one public prosecutor should be there for each court for all working days. Necessary training must also be given to all the public prosecutors time to time to keep update them from latest development of law. There is also huge **shortage of stenographers and trained clerks** all across the state of Gujarat which causes hurdle in timely delievry of Justice. While recruiting these staff members, priority be given to persons of legal background.

Another considerable aspect is **Process/Summons Serving agency, doubtless, plays a crucial role** in the pendency of cases and reportedly, they handle their job somewhat mechanically. Earnest efforts are not being made by the police in executing summon or warrant efficiently or in apprehending and producing the absocnding accused or out of state accused for their own reasons- genuine as well as artificial.

Police even fail to ensure that prosecution witnesses turn up in time and quite often, even Investing officers are defaulters. Trial cases are adjourned quite often for non-appearance of witnesses. If the accused or witness has changed the address it should be informed to the court at the earliest. Otherwise, repetedly process will be issued without any fruitful result and an already old case become more and more infrctuous and dead-wood. A little amount of understanding effort on their part is likely to go on long to improve the response of the public and their willingness to cooperate in the administration of justice and also result in less burden on them in future. Otherwise, a seperate investigating agency for the courts remains only remedy.

3. Outdated Infrastructure & limited computerization-Poor infrastructure in courts and absence of computerized records and use of information technology etc. amounts to considerable bottleneck in prompt disposal of cases. This is age of technology, today even the smallest office in private sector is well equipped with computerized record and proceedings, which help them to raise their efficiency and update their records.

Though, recently, the Judiciary has also been provided with electronic devices like laptops, printers, softwares and fax etc.. But almost all the courts have heaps of rotten files in the basement and computerization of record has remained an unsolved issue. In many courts, the court building itself is not sufficient to accomodate as per required norms. A lot of considerable time is spent in manually dealing with court process. Thus, as we are living in the age of information technology, yet our methodologies are outdated and restricted only to limited computerization and urgently need a re-look. Like western countries, digitalized secured issuance of process (summon, warrant etc.) directly to process serving agency by use of information technology, can easily solve all the issues relating to non-service of process, particularly in cases where the accused or witnesses resde out of district or state. It will be very much useful if all the police stations and linked stations can be linked with a computerized network, so that the processes of persons residing out of district and out of state can be directly send to concerned police station or link station. Even some littile use of technology in present system like- <u>use of mobile number</u> of accused and witnesses for informing them directly of required presence can be very useful.

4. Neglect of Old Cases-

For the purpose of academic discussion, we here consider a criminal case as old if it is not disposed within one year of filling of chargesheet. Now, in a new case, the witnesses and accused are readily available and hence, the process serving agency has to invest small effort in securing their presence in the court whereas it is not so in the old cases. Further, the Muddamal, production papers, suriety etc. all are availalble in new cases whereas it is not necessary so in old cases.

The approach and co-operation of advocates and process service agency is also positive in new cases. But it is not so in old cases. The real reason behind the huge backlog of old criminal cases is that necessary attention and priority is given only to new cases rather than old cases in present justice delievry system and as a result an old case becomes critical old in future.

Under the present assessment policy and the promotion policy which is discussed in the matter of **Vinay Kumar v. High Court of Gujarat**[23], the judges gets involved in the race of disposal of cases and quite often they assume that the object and need of law is speedy disposal alone. The same is evident from poor conviction ratio itself. But the real object of Law is 'Speedy and fair justice'. 'Justice hurried is justice worried' is eually considerable phenomenon than 'Justice delayed is justice denied'. A proper balanced approach is required to be maintained by judicial officers while handling judicial work. While saying so, it is also the need of the hour that present assessment policy be substituted with a **'Career Advancement Scheme (CAS)'** under which priority be always given to 'qualiity of justice' rather than 'quantity of justice' and the judicial work should be allotted to Judges as per their area of specialization/interest. The assessment should be done according to nature and criticalness of the case, number of witnesses testified etc. as the task of disposal of old criminal cases is not only time-consuming but includes a lot of mental exercise and extra labour too. The Presiding Officer has to wade

---
[23] SLP No. 8793 of 2015 decided on 15/07/2015

through the labyrinths of the voluminous record which has swollen in course of time on account of continued long pendency. So, the old cases should be categorized in 'old', 'very old' and 'critically old category' and filled accordingly and additional assessment weightage be provided to Judges according to category of criminal cases as suggested in the matter of **Siddhartha Kumar And Others vs Upper Civil Judge[24]**.

5. Frequent Adjournment Applications-

An advocate is an important and integral part of justice delivery system. It is the role and responsibility of an advocate to identify and clarify factual issues relating to the side of the case he representing and provide necessary information and support to his client as well as to the Court. But unfortunately, today the term 'advocate' and 'adjournment' are running parelel to each-ther. The advocates files adjournment applications and miscellaneous applications even for triffling issues which can be ordinarily taken care with.

---

[24] 1998 (1) AWC 593.

An immunity is also granted to the advocates under the system that prayer in their application need not required to be specific or even supported with some evidence or documents. As a result, instead of prompt hearing, such miscellaneous applications are fixed for hearing and the routine hearing of the case is sidelined.

No doubt an adovate is under professional duty to represent in the interest of his client but he also has his professional commitment towards the Court also. They must always come well prepared in the court and provide necessary information and support to judges in the work of departing timely justice to the parties rather than asking time for preparation and thereby prolonging the case. The courts run in two shifts and hence, even preparation is required or there is some other workloads, they should show thier willingness to plead thier side in the second shift or on a nearby day.

The Judges should also deal such applications as per mandate of law rather than the comfort of lawyers. Both the Judges and the advocates must remember that 'there is an overflowing grace, for every great work'.

There are other factors also which are contributory for the delay in the disposal of cases. It is expected from the Judges that they will dispense justice in a cool, peaceful atmosphere. Due to the attitude of certain members of the Bar not only the disposal of the cases is delayed but it puts the judicial officers under mental strain. Sometimes the atmosphere of the court rooms is so hot up that mental equilibrium of thejudicial officers is unnecessarily disturbed. It has been observed by the Apex Court in K P. Tewari v. State of M. P.[25] that it has also to be remembered that the lower Judicial officers mostly work under a charged atmosphere and are constantly under a psychological pressure with all the contestants and their lawyers almost breathing down their necks, more correctly up to their nostrils.[26]

6. Strikes by Advocates

In a country where rule of law prevails and is a basic feature of our Constitution disputes are required to be resolved not by taking them to street but by bringing them for adjudication by a competent and Impartial Judge functioning in the court.

---

[25] AIR 1994 SC 103.

[26] Siddhartha Kumar And Others vs Upper Civil Judge, Senior Division, Para 7, 1998 (1) AWC 593.

Strike by lawyers is. therefore, very negation of this basic concept. It is obvious that strike or boycott by lawyers or absence of lawyers from the court in the name of one issue or the other has resulted in adding to the already existing back breaking burden. Taking public opinion and pursuading the local faternity to see this problem in the right perspective is no doubt one way of tackling this problem. Though such attempts were attempted the problem very much exists and it is virtually getting out of control as lawyers go on strike all over the country on even smallest provocations. The lawyers who hold the briefs for their clients when they resolve to delay the disposal of their cases or allow their case to be dismissed for default, betray not only the trust reposed by their respective client but also confidence which the courts repose in the legal profession.[27]

- **Procedural Bottlenecks in Disposal of Old Criminal Cases-**

Though, Human and material resource can be one factor, but dilatory procedures may be an equal causative factor for delays in disposal of criminal cases.

---
[27]Mallmath Committee Report, Page 42.

Thus, unless the procedural bottlenecks are identified and solved, merely alleging the human and material resources cannot achieve speedy justice. Therefore, it will be worthwhile to look into depth some procedural bottlenecks in disposal of old criminal cases outlined by the Gujarat State Judicial Academy-

(a) Non-service of Process to Accused and witnesses-

In old criminal cases proper implementation of process is an key issue and therefore, a presiding officer must involve himself in the process of issuing summons, warrants etc. Sometimes, the proper and complete address is not mentioned which resuts in failure of appearance of the desired person. When a presiding officer himself issues important processses and moniters them, he becomes familiar with the facts and circumstances and accordingly he can ensure proper steps for appearance of the accused and he can evolve his own methodology as well. Sometimes so happens that the accused disappears and not readily available. in these circumstances, his surety or previous advocate who secured his bail or the I.O. of the case can be called and through that via media his appearance can be secured.

Another important bottleneck relating to delay in old cases is that the **bail-bond papers are missing** and therefore neighther the accused nor does the surety can be traced. In this regard, help can be taken from the advocate who ensured bail for the accused and if the accused was released on bail from police station, a list of such cases can be sent to officer incharge of the police station for doing required in the interest of justice. The investigating officer of such cases, if he is present in some other case or otherwise, his help can also be taken. **Accused of many old cases are of outside state** and in such cases the language of process becomes the paramount consideration. upto the extent possible english and the local language of the state should be given priority in such cases. Endoresement behind returned process should also be understood in proper manner. The P.S.I. of the concerned police station and his subordinates should be made aware regarding the mandate of the appex as well as high court and district court regarding priority to old cases and for that process can be sent with endorsement of old case and along with letter. 'A rolling stone gethers no moss' is the key formula here. if process are served sometime but not regularly, all the efferots will be useless. hence, the presiding officer should absolutely ensure that every time process are issued in right direction so as to achieve the goal. while doing so the presiding officer should keep in mind one age old formula- 'where there is will, there is a way.'

(b) cases of accused of unsound mind.

In this regard, special procedure for accused persons of unsound mind has been laid under the Code of Criminal Procedure[28] and the same should be implemented in its letter and spirit so as not to be confused or mix such cases with regular cases and thereby causing further delay and ultimately injustice with the persons concerned in the case. It should also be taken care that no accused person illegly took shelter of these provisions to run away from grips of legal machinary.

(c) Bed ridden/Serious illness of witnesses or accused.

If the accused person is serious ill and thereby cannot attend the court, his personal attendence can be dispensed with and with presence of his advocate the case can be proceeded further.

---

[28] Section 328 to 339 of the Chapter XXV of the Code of Criminal Procedure.

If there is serious question of his identification, that portion of evidence can be postponed by a clear note/order and meanwhile other evidence can be taken and the identification evidence can be taken lateron when the accused will be fit. Similarly, if a witness is ill and not able to attend the court at a particular point of time, there is no logic in just waiting for his presence, the court should move further with other available evience. All applications filed on medical ground including the seek notes of advocates should be supported with medical documents.

(d) Loss of police papers, original documents or deposition etc.

If any police paper important for trial like complaint, panchnama or statement of witnesses which was submitted to court at the time of filling chargesheet is lost, its duplicate can be obtained from the prosecution file. Regarding question of loss of original document, there are provisions in law of evidence for secondary evidence where primary is not available. With relevant endorsement of ld. Adv. of accused, secondary evidence can be exhibited and included in evidence.

If a witness is already deposed but his deposition is not available, by making necessary note and information to required persons & after following due process, witness can be recalled and his deposition can be secured.

(e) Loss or non-production of mudammal.

Loss of mudamal happens only in exceptional cases as mudammal is kept in safe custody of police or nazir etc. but even if so happens, it attracts departmental inquiry. Non-production of muddamal can definately be handled by effective Court management and case management. Adjournment of case just for non-production of muddamal also shakes image of the court and hence a presiding officer of the court be very aware and alert regarding every stage of the case. In most of the case, mudammal is required at the time of testimony of complainant or injured witnesses.

While issuing summon to such witnesses, notice for producing muddammal should also be sent simultaneously to the police station, so that the matter will not be unnecessariy adjourned for the want of identification of muddamal or for its non-production.

The concerned clerk also be directed to cheque compliance of all procedural formalities a day earlier of scheduled board.

(f) non-proceeding due to deposition is illegible, torn or remained unsigned.

'Prevention is better than cure' is the perfect remedy for such sort of bottlenecks. It is true that the concerned clerk has to right speedily, the deposition narrated in the court but if it is not legible, it can give birth to a lot of mutual contradictory interpretations which is certainly not in the interest of the justice. Therefore, the presiding offficer must ensure that a person having good handwritting or at least legible handwritting is assigned duty of writting depositions and upto extent possible, effort should be made to type the deposition on computer rather than traditional handwritting manner. Typing deposition on computer also saves time in case of repetation and the same can directly be used at the time of writting orders or judgements. If the deposition is recorded by a judicial officer who is now transfered and due to some reason it has remained unsigned, by obtaining no objection of both the side & with required noting, it can be signed post-dated.

(g) non-commital of sessions cases-

Sessions cases are more serious in nature compared to other cases. Section 193 of the Code of Criminal procedure mandates that the Court of session cannot take cognizance of any offence unless the case has been committed to it by the concerned magistrate after complying with necesssary formalities. It is the statutory duty of the magistrate to comply with the necessary formalities like- muddamal, bail-bond, documents and presence of all the accused and obtain required Pursis and commit the case to the sessions court at the earliest. The date so fixed must also be expressly informed to the parties so that further proceedings can be strated smoothly at the sessions court level.

(h) cases stayed or record and proceedings called by higher forum-

The record of the trial court is often summoned by the higher court for the purposes of disposal of an appeal or revision and other miscellaneous matters. Sometimes such R&P continues to gather dust and are shelved in the office of the higher courts for a much longer period than is required.

Even though the stay order or interim order has not been granted or granted but vacated, the trial court cannot proceed with the case unless the original record summoned by the higher court is received back by it. Therefore, while deciding the appeals, revisions or other miscellaneous proceedings. It would be proper and necessary if the appellate or revisional court while pronouncing the Judgment, fixes a date on which both the parties may be , required to appear before the trial court. In that event, at least one of the parties would appear before the court below and it may bring to its notice that no further proceedings are pending before the higher court. The court below would then pursue the matter to get back the record from the higher court. The appellate or revisional courts at the district level should ensure that the record of the decided cases are immediately transmitted back to the trial courts.

(i) Retirement of complainant or Winding up of accused company-Sometimes, presence of the goverment servents involved in a case as witnesses like complainants, investigating officers, medical officers or others of like nature becomes a tuff task as they are often transfered or retired.

In old cases, it is a serious bottleneck. The Hon'ble Supreme Court and High Courts have repetedly observed in various judgments that it is the duty of the investing officer to ensure that the required witnesses are kept pesence for evidence. The process service agency here appears to be not working with the e-communication methods like-fax, telephonic communication and even social media tools like whats-up etc., at least to ensure presence of govt. servant presence in old cases of urgent nature.Regarding winding up of company, procedure is to be dealt now according to provisions of the new Company Act. Procedural aspect relating to liability of concerned directors/managerial persons is normal as per ordinary accused.

Thus, it can be seen that improved efficiency and productivity in Judiciary is the need of the hour. Honest efforts must be made by the Bar, the Bench and the Government to strengthen the pillar of justice. In spite of so many ills which plague our judicial system, the overflowing docket of court cases is a positive sign of people's faith in the judiciary.

We may make the best laws and introduce new procedures, yet it may not have done enough to achieve the constitutional promise of providing justice. Remeber-" The best practice is one which results in justice."

Chapter 3
DOCTRINE OF 'TRIAL IN ABSENTIA

1. Background

It is often seen that non-appearance of accused in large number of cases is deliberate to evade trial which eventually delays criminal adjudication and causes multiplicity of cases[29]. The right of an accused to watch the prosecution witnesses deposing before a court of law indisputably iS a valuable right.

The Sixth Amendment of the United States Constitution explicitly provides therefore, which reads that in all criminal prosecutions, the accused shall enjoy the right to a speedy and public trial, by an impartial jury of the State and district wherein the crime shall have been committed, which district shall have been previously ascertained by law, and to be informed of the nature and cause of the accusation; to be confronted with the witnesses against him; to have compulsory process for obtaining witnesses in his favour, and to have the assistance of counsel for his defense.[30]

---

[29] As different cases arises out of one incidence against different absconding accused.
[30] Jayendra Vishnu Thakur Vs State of Maharastra and another (2009) 7 SCC 104.

In a situation of deliberate non-appearance of the accused[31] to evade the trial, the victim suffers a huge loss and their years long wait for justice stumbls the faith of the people. But the Criminal Procedure Code mandates the presence of accused at all the stages of trial whether it is the stage of commital, evidence of witnesses, recording of further stament or the judgement.[32]

There are express provisions for taking evidence in absence of the accused.[33] Section 299 of Code of Criminal Procedure is main provision to meet exigency of abscondance-

"**299. Record of evidence in absence of accused.**
(1) If it is proved that an accused person has absconded, and that there is no immediate prospect of arresting him, the Court competent to try, or commit for trial such person for the offence complained of may, in his absence, examine the witnesses (if any) produced on behalf of the prosecution, and record their depositions and any such deposition may, on the arrest of such person, be given in evidence against him on the inquiry into, or trial for, the offence with which he is charged, if the deponent is dead or incapable of giving evidence or cannot be found or his presence cannot be procured without an amount of-delay, expense or inconvenience which, under the circumstances of the case, would be unreasonable.

---

[31] Whether at pre-charge stage or post-charge stage.
[32] Section 273 of Cr.P.C. particularly requires that the evidence is to be recorded in the presence of the accused.
[33]Sections 284, 291, 292, 293 and 299 of Cr.P.C.

(2) If it appears that an offence punishable with death or imprisonment for life has been committed by some person or persons unknown, the High Court or the Sessions Judge may direct that any Magistrate of the first class shall hold an inquiry and examine any witnesses who can give evidence concerning the offence and any depositions so taken may be given in evidence against any person who is subsequently accused of the offence, if the deponent is dead or incapable of giving evidence or beyond the limits of India."

Clearly, the language in which above provision is cauched is ineffective in its present form, it is dilatory in its procedure of declaring absconder, it is non-productive since even after the recording the evidence in absentia the same can not be used unless giving a right of crossexamination to the accused, if the witness is alive etc., it puts a premium to abscond and scuttle the trial and plead for the right to confront the witnesses already examined in his absence, whenever the accused is arrested.

The issue of bringing to justice an offender who has absconded is not of our nation only but the Courts world over are facing it and many countries have adopted, whether fully or in part, Doctrine of Trail in absentia as a plausible solution of it.

Certain countries like US, England, Canada Australia, New Zealand and other nations now do not recognize an absolute right of the accused to confront the witness and it can be deemed to be waived in the event of their willful absconding.

- **Origin and Development of Doctrine**

The anglo-american criminal jurisprudence holds that in normal trial, the accused is represented by his counsel and during trial his presence can be dispense with as well. Similarly, the presence and identification of the accused can be dispensed when the accused absconds and the trial can be proceeded in absentia. Therefore, this Doctrine casts a burden of the accused to remain present during trial to defend himself in his own interest.As early as in year 1901, in the matter of **The Falk v. United States**[34] , the accused though remained present at the stage of commencement of the trial but after grant of bail absconded. The court held that it does not seem consonant with the dictates of common sense that an accused person, being at large upon bail, should be at liberty, whenever he pleases, to withdraw himself from the courts of his country and to break up a trial already commenced.

---

[34] 181 U.S. 618 (1901).

In 1912, the U.S. Supreme Court while dealing with Doctrine of 'trial in absentia' in **Diaz v. United States**[35], held that where the offence is not capital and the accused is not in custody, the prevailing rule has been that if, after the trial has begun in his presence, he voluntarily absents himself, this does not nullify what has been done or prevent the completion of trial, but, on the contrary, operates as a waiver of his right to be present and leaves the court free to proceed with the trial in like manner and with like effect as if he were present. In the matter of **R v. Jones**[36], the European Courts also adopted the doctrine and observed that the English courts are intact in adopting the doctrine of 'trial in absentia' in conditions where the accused deliberately attempts to evade trial by way of abscondance. Not only English courts, the countries such as Canada, Australia and New Zealand also appreciated the problem of deliberate non-appearance by way of adoption of doctrine of trial in absentia. Bangladesh legislation is a classic example of the dynamic approach needed for criminal legislations to avoid a situation of control of defendant over the criminal trial.

---

[35] 223 U.S. 442 (1912).

[36] 1972 2 All E R 731.

- **Trial in absentia under International Law**

Under International Law, as a general rule, a defendent's presence during trial is considered as fundamental to due process. In this regard, **International Covenant on civil and political rights (ICCPR)** specifically provides:

"In the determination of any criminal charge against him, everyone shall be entitled to the following minimum guarantees, in full equality:

….(d) To be tried in his presence, and to defend himself in person or through legal assistance of his own choosing; to be informed, if he does not have legal assistance, of this right; and to have legal assistance assigned to him, in any case where the interests of justice so require, and without payment by him in any such case if he does not have sufficient means to pay for it."[37]

Further, General Comment No. 13 of the **UN Human Rights Committee ("UNHRC")** states-

"The accused or his lawyer must have the right to act diligently and fearlessly in pursuing all available defenses and the right to challenge the conduct of the case if they believe it to be unfair. When exceptionally for justified reasons trials in absentia are held, strict observance of the rights of the defense is all the more necessary."[38]

---

[37]International Covenant on Civil and Political Rights, Article 14(3)(b), Dec.19,1966, 999 UNTS 171, 6 ILM 368. (hereinafter ICCPR)

[38]Office of the High Commissioner for Human rights, Human rights commission, 21st sess., Article 14, 11, HRI/GEN/1/Rev.9(Vol.1)(Apr1.13, 1984)

However, General Comment No. 13 of UNHRC does not prescribes 'justified reasons'. In **Mbenge v. Zaire**,[39] the UNHRC shed some light on the particular circumstances that could justify a trial in absentia:

"According to Article 14(3) of the Covenant, everyone is entitled to be tried in his presence and to defend himself in person or through legal assistance. This provision and other requirements of due process enshrined in Article 14 cannot be construed as invariably rendering proceedings in absentia inadmissible, irrespective of the reasons for the accused person's absence. Indeed, proceedings in absentia are in some circumstances (for instance, when the accused person, although informed of the proceedings sufficiently in advance, declines to exercise his right to be present) permissible in the interest of the proper administration of justice.

- **Nature of Waiver**

It can be seen that the early cases gave little consideration to the nature of the waiver imputed to a defendant who voluntarily absented himself from his trial. When the defendant absented himself temporarily and consented that the trial proceed in his absence, there was, of course, an express waiver."[40]

---

[39] U.N. Human Rights Comm., Mbenge v. Zaire, U.N. Doc. CCPR/C/OP/2 (Mar. 25, 1983).
[40] Diaz v. United States, 223 U.S. 442 (1912).

When, on the other hand, the defendant became a fugitive after the commencement of trial, most of the cases seemed to rule that he had lost the right to be present as a matter of policy.[41] However, the United States Supreme Court has often discussed the law of waiver and prescribed strict standards which must be met before a waiver of constitutional rights will be found-at least as to those rights which guarantee a fair trial and protect the reliability of the truth-finding process.[42] It is well settled, for example, that the courts indulge every reasonable presumption against the waiver of such rights.[43] It is further settled that a waiver of such a right must be "an intentional relinquishment or abandonment of a known right or privilege. All of this means, as the Court has stated: "Waivers of constitutional rights not only must be voluntary but must be knowing, intelligent acts done with sufficient awareness of the relevant circumstances and likely consequences."[44]

---

[41]Falk v. United States, 15 App. D.C. 446, 460 (1899),

[42]Schneckloth v. Bustamonte, 412 U.S. 218, 235-37 (1973).

[43] Johnson v. Zerbst, 304 U.S. 458, 464 (1938). But cf. Schneckloth v. Bustamonte, 412 U.S. 218 (1973) (upholding a consent search). In that case, the Court noted: "[U]nlike those constitutional guarantees that protect a defendant at trial, it cannot be said every reasonable presumption ought to be indulged against voluntary relinquishment [of fourth amendment rights]." Id. at 243.

[44]Brady v. United States, 397 U.S. 742, 748 (1970).

- **Procedural Safeguards-**

Subject to procedural safeguards, trials in absentia are permitted in certain prescribed circumstances. These safeguards can be summarized as follows:

(i) The accused must have knowledge of the indictment and proceedings (which must be demonstrated by the prosecution), and voluntarily chooses to be absent from the hearings and unequivocally states this to the court;

(ii) The accused must have unequivocally stated to the court that he waives his right to be present at court but by his behavior implies that he waives his right to be present e.g., when a defendant is absconding;

(iii) The defendant has been expelled from the courtroom for disruption or misconduct.

In the first set of circumstances, a trial in absentia can be held provided that the accused has been duly informed of the proceedings and has unequivocally refused to be present during her trial. A defendant's silence after attempted notice does not constitute a waiver.[45]

---

[45] Colozza v. Italy, App. No. 9024/80, Eur. Ct. H.R., ¶ 28 (1985).

In the final set of circumstances, the ECtHR most recently held that when a defendant's behavior is disruptive to the extent that the court deems it necessary to expel him from the courtroom, the presiding judge should "establish that the applicant could have reasonably foreseen what the consequences of his ongoing conduct would be prior to her decision to order his removal from the courtroom." This can be done by issuing a warning or allowing for a short adjournment to permit the defendant an opportunity to consider the consequences of his action and to compose himself.[46]

Thus, it can be seen that The jurisprudence of both the ICCPR and the ECHR confirms that a trial in absentia will not violate a person's right to be present when he has expressly declined to exercise this right. The circumstance and the time and way the accused had gone to absconsion and left country led us to lawful inference that the accused has expressly declined to exercise his right to be present in trial.

---

[46] Idalov v. Russia, App. No. 5826/03, Eur. Ct. H.R. (2012), available at http://hudoc.echr.coe.int/sites/eng/pages/search.aspx?i=001-110986 (citing Jones v. the United Kingdom, No. 30900/02, Eur. Ct. H.R. (2003), available at http://hudoc.echr.coe.int/sites/eng/pages/search.aspx?i=001-23360).

Chapter 4
Bottlenecks in Disposal of Old Civil Cases

The judicial system in India is set to expand significantly over the next three decades, rising, by the most conservative estimate, to at least about 15 crore of cases requiring at least some 75,000 Judges. At present, there are 14.95 lakh criminal cases and 5.89 lakh civil cases are pending in District courts in Gujarat and arround 24% of the cases are over 10 years old. In statewise pendency of old cases, the Gujarat secures its place in top six states. The Civil Law is such which has a very wide scope for delaying the trial of the suit and everytime the matter comes on board, the Court has to deal with various kinds of applications and under the circumstances, the matter is surely delayed because the Court cannot decide the application without hearing the parties and it has to give time to the other side to file reply or for hearing of the application.

The Judge can only bear in the mind the circulars and directions for speedily disposal of such old civil cases but under the system, such old civil suits becomes 'critically old civil case' in future.

Therefore, there is an urgent need to achieve speedy justice by shortening the average life cycle of civil cases and to enhance the quality of justice in such bulky and contested old civil cases by addressing the bottlenecks in disposal of old civil cases.

1. Bottlenecks in Disposal of Old Civil Cases-

Some common bottlenecks in disposal of old cases like- Poor judge population ratio, lack of sufficient and efficient manpower, outdated ifrastructure and limited computerization, neglect of old cases and adjournment applications are already discussed in my first article and hence they are not rediscussed here. It will be worthwhile to look into depth some procedural bottlenecks in disposal of old civil cases outlined by the Gujarat State Judicial Academy-

*(a) **Non-service of process -***

When the suit is instituted before the Court, the procedure is that process is issued to the defendant upon payment of process fee by the plaintiff. Many times, the process fee is not paid by the plaintiff and the matter kept pending for payment of process fee.

Many times, the process is returned without service due to wrong address of the party or the party has left the place or has gone abroad. In such a situation, the matter remains pending for the address of the defendant which is to be submitted by the plaintiff. The Civil Procedure Code has provided various form and manner for service of process like- service by affixation, substituted service etc. The party can also apply to the Court for service of process through registered post. Further, the service can be made upon the advocate for the party also (if he has appeared) under Rule 3 to Order III of C.P.C. Many times, the process does not return with or without service specifically when the summons is sent for service outside the jurisdiction of the Court. In such cases, the summon should be sent to the court having jurisdiction on that territory for service and such court directs its serving officer to serve the process and return the same as speedily as possible. Elaborate provisions relating to service of process in civil cases are laid down in Section 27, 28, 29, 143 and Order V (Rules 9 to 30), Order XXVII(Rule 4), Order XXIX(Rule 2), Order XLVIII (Rules 1, 2 and 3), Order III(Rules 3, 5 and 6), Order XXVIII(Rule3), Order XXX(Rule 3), and Order XLI(Rule 14)of the Code of Civil Procedure and the same ae required to be implemented in their letter and spirit. Some of these provisions have been amended by Amendment Acts in 1999 and 2002 to tackle the problem of delays in court processes. The provisions that have undergone amendments are mentioned below:

1. As per section 27, the summons may be served on such day not beyond thirty days from the date of the institution of suit.

2. Order V Rule 1 which also deals with service of summons has been amended and states that no service of summons is necessary in case where the defendant has appeared at the time of presentation of the plaint and admitted the petitioners claim. Amendment has further added a proviso that the defendant has to file his written statement within thirty days from the date of service of summons and if the defendant fails to file the same within the prescribed period, the court may extend the time but not more than ninety days for the reasons to be recorded in writing.

3. Rule 9 Order V deals with delivery of summons by court. This Rule as amended in 2002, mandates delivery has to be either through proper officer or by post acknowledgment due or by speed post or through an approved courier, fax, email.
4. Rule 9-A provides service could also be done by plaintiff by taking delivery of summons from the court and tendering the same to the defendant personally or by Fax, courier, email etc.
5. Rule 9 Sub Rule 4 provides service of summons on a defendant residing outside the territorial jurisdiction of that court through any one of the courier services approved by it. An improvement over the 1999 Act insofar as the local court has now got power to approve the courier service, whereas earlier only the high courts had the power to do so. The decentralization would speed up the process of service.

6. Order IX Rule 2 provides dismissal of suit where summons are not served in consequence of plaintiff's failure to pay costs. Where on the day fixed for hearing it is found that on the failure of the plaintiff to file process fee or pay court fee or any other reason attributable to the plaintiff, service has not been affected on the defendant, the court may dismiss the suit.

(b) Non farming of Issue:-

The huge workload on the Courts results into lack of time and many times the Presiding Officer is not be able to timely frame the issues because of burden of other case. The code of civil procedure provides that the issue be frammed in consulation with the advocates and while considering moel issues provided by them. But unfortunately, the advocates do not even remain present on the date fixed for framming of issues and do not provide necessary support to the court in this task.

Therefore, the best option is that if there is an temporary injunction (Exh. 5) application pending, while deciding such application the Judge should frame the issues as well as that time he is well versed with the facts and circumstances of the suit. If there is no such application, in such a case, the day or at least a shift of day (probably post lunch) should be fixed with the target for framing the issues only so that issues are timely frammed and delay does not happen due to non framing of issues. Further, the issues shall be framed giving priority to oldest cases first. The Gujarat State Judicial Academy has also published and circulated a guide of model issues in various suits which is very much useful and it must be circulated again for all the judges again.

(c) Frequent Interlocutory and Miscellaneous Applications -

The Code of Civil Procedure is a complete code in itself and it enumerates subtantive procedure in the first part in section and also the detailed procedure in the second part in Orders.

Any advocate for the party who wishes to delay the proceedings can move any interim or miscellaneous application like Joining of legal heirs/adding or deleting of party, production of document, return/rejection of plaint, amendment of plaint etc. and the suit will be delayed due to want of deciding those applications first. The Judge is duty bound to hear and decide the same on merits. Such frequently filed applications are the main cause for delay in disposal of civil suits. While dealing with such applications, the role of a judge becomes equal to a research scholar.

The Judge must immediately try to identify the nature of remedy sought, the mandate of law, interpretation provided by hon'ble higher courts and the interest of parties and than pass a rational order. If the Judge finds such an application without merits, such an application shall be rejected with costs so as to prevent filing of such applications in future.

If required, help can be taken from senior officers as well. Learning is an endless process and even judges are no exception.

(d) Non proceeding due to deposition is illegible, torn. Lost or remained unsigned:-

'Prevention is better than cure' is the perfect remedy for such sort of bottlenecks. It is true that the concerned clerk has to right speedily, the deposition narrated in the court but if it is not legible, it can give birth to a lot of mutual contradictory interpretations which is certainly not in the interest of the justice.

Therefore, the presiding offficer must ensure that a person having good handwritting or at least legible handwritting is assigned duty of writting depositions and upto extent possible, effort should be made to type the deposition on computer rather than traditional handwritting manner. Typing deposition on computer also saves time in case of repetation and the same can directly be used at the time of writting orders or judgements.

If the deposition is recorded by a judicial officer who is now transfered and due to some reason it has remained unsigned, by obtaining no objection of both the side & with required noting, it can be signed post-dated.

The Judges, while recording the deposition should take care that the deposition is signed after the same has been taken down and the staff should be directed to write the deposition properly and to keep it with the record in such a way that it does not get lost or does not tear.

(e) Case Stayed or record and proceeding called by higher forum:-

The record of the trial court is often summoned by the higher court for the purposes of disposal of an appeal or revision and other miscellaneous matters. Sometimes such R&P continues to gather dust and are shelved in the office of the higher courts for a much longer period than is required. Even though the stay order or interim order has not been granted or granted but vacated, the trial court cannot proceed with the case unless the original record summoned by the higher court is received back by it. Therefore, while deciding the appeals, revisions or other miscellaneous proceedings.

It would be proper and necessary if the appellate or revisional court while pronouncing the Judgment, fixes a date on which both the parties may be , required to appear before the trial court.

In that event, at least one of the parties would appear before the court below and it may bring to its notice that no further proceedings are pending before the higher court. The court below would then pursue the matter to get back the record from the higher court. The appellate or revisional courts at the district level should ensure that the record of the decided cases are immediately transmitted back to the trial courts. In such cases, both the parties should cooperate with the Appellate Court to dispose of the matter so that the lower Court can try the matter speedily and the matter can be disposed of quickly.

(f) Trial of case is dependent on the decision of other govt. agencies viz. Tenancy Act, Fragmentation Act:-

Many times, the decision of the particular is remains pending as the decision relating to the subject matter is pending in the other revenue department of government and the departments are not interested in carrying out the civil cases early. This is the common reason for pendency of many such civil suits .

(g) Approach of parties to prolong the matters:-

Parties are best known to the actual reality and the facts of their cases. It is always a rule that a party wins and other loses. The party who is well versed with the fact that it has a bad case, always try to prolong the matter and will try to delay the proceedings. Non-appearance of parties or witnesses, unpreparedness of the defence advocate or prosecutor, non-availability of time of the court, non-availability of lower court records or copies of documents and the like are the common grounds on which adjournments ara often sought and granted. Such a party keeps submitting various kinds of application for delaying the trail of the case like submitting an interim application for adding or striking out party, submitting an application for interlocutory injunction, submitting an application under Order VII Rule 11 of Civil Procedure Code, etc. Such applications delay the trial of the suit. Moreover, if the Court, taking all measures, disposes of the civil suit on merits, then the party tries to delay the execution proceedings of the same suit by submitting various objections pertaining to jurisdiction, etc.

In such a case, the Court is helpless and has to hear the applications submitted by the party and decide the suit on merits. The Court can only try to decide such application with urgent hearing on such application so as to reach the conclusion and dispose the suit.

(h) Approach of of presiding judges to deal old cases:-

(i) non-implemention of procedural law i.e Sec. 89, Order 10, 11, 12, 15, 16, 16A etc of CPC:- The provisions regarding first hearing is not applied in actual practice. If the Court direct each party to give full details of his claim to title and possession as required under O10 CPC together with discovery, production and admission/denial of all document (Order 11 and 12) and then pending trial, call for security for costs and ultimately while deciding the matter not miss out on the mesne profits, costs and penalties (Sections 34,35 CPC), including a prison term to one who resorted to a false suit on the basis of a false affidavit or forged document (s/340Cr.P.C) the unscrupulous litigation to a large extent will be Checked.

(ii) Norms and assessment and preference to criminal work:- Under the present assessment policy and the promotion policy which is discussed in the matter of **Vinay Kumar v. High Court of Gujarat**, SLP No. 8793 of 2015 decided on 15/07/2015, the judges gets involved in the race of disposal of cases and in the number game. The real reason behind the huge backlog of old civil cases is that necessary attention and priority is given only to new cases and criminal case rather than old civil cases in present justice delievry system and as a result an old civil case becomes critical old in future. A proper balanced approach is required to be maintained by judicial officers while handling judicial work. While saying so, it is also the need of the hour that present assessment policy be substituted with a 'Career Advancement Scheme (CAS)' under which priority be always given to 'qualiity of justice' rather than 'quantity of justice' and the judicial work should be allotted to Judges as per their area of specialization/interest. The assessment should be done according to nature and criticalness of the case, number of witnesses testified, number of interlocutory applications and miscellaneous applications decided etc. The judges are appointed at a station for three years and quite often they do not show interest in proceeding further with the suit because they think that they will not be able to dispose o f the suit in their remaining tenure. As the task of disposal of old civil cases is not only time-consuming but includes a lot of mental exercise and extra labour too and he Presiding Officer has to wade through the labyrinths of the voluminous record which has swollen in course of time on account of continued long pendency, the assessment should also be provided according to number of stages passed in the suit. The old civil cases must also be categorized in 'old', 'very old' and 'critically old category' and filled accordingly and additional assessment weightage be provided to Judges according to category of criminal cases as suggested in the matter of **Siddhartha Kumar And Others vs Upper Civil Judge**, 1998 (1) AWC 593.

(i) Unequal distribution of work and lack of monitoring work load:-

This is the most common problem in working of the Courts in the state of Gujarat. Work has been unequally distributed among the Judges.

In a Court, there are around 1000 files whereas another Court in the same premises will have 2000 files. This problem arises because the institution has been given to a single Court and when the institution of matters is with a single Court, the instituting Court will have more work than the other Courts and such a Court would be more effective in disposal of cases. Further, the Judges in many districts have so much burden of cases whereas, the Judges in other district does not much cases so that they can get the proper disposal as per the norms. This is required to be taken into consideration while transferring the Judges from one place to another. In big cities like Ahmedabad, Vadodara, Rajkot, etc, where the burden of cases is much, more Judges are required to be appointed at such place for proper disposal of case.

(I) Government litigation- Inadequacy, Commitment to work, Knowledge of AGP etc.:-

In such suits where the government is one of the parties, such suits remains pending in the state for long time at different levels. The reason being the AGPs are not available in the Courts and if available, they are not attending the Courts regularly.

Such civil suits can be decided only when the adequate number of AGPs are appointed and they cooperate in the disposal of the suits.

(K) Data grid, NCMS, SCMS:-

The Government has introduced Data Grid system all over the country to track pendency and disposal of cases in each and every Court. It is useful for the person who travels long distance for the purpose of getting the next date of hearing. With the use of this online data grid system, every report pertaining to the cases and Courts is available online. Further, the National Court Management System (NCMS), State Court Management System (SCMS) are related with the administration of justice. The object of NCMS is to lower the pendency of the cases in Courts to "5+0" i.e. the cases which are more than five years old should be disposed of. Hon'ble Mr. Justice S. H. Kapadia, Former Chief Justice of India, came with the ide of NCMS in the year 2006. National Court Management System (NCMS) was established under the overall control of Hon'ble the Chief Justice of India for enhancing timely justice in the country.

The Scheme provides six main elements to include in the system which are:

1. A National Framework of Court Excellence (NFCE) that will set measurable **performance standards** for Indian courts, addressing issues of quality, responsiveness and timeliness.

2. A system for **monitoring** and enhancing the performance parameters established in the NFCE on quality, responsiveness and timeliness.

3. A system of **Case Management** to enhance user friendliness of the Judicial System.

4. A **National System of Judicial Statistics (NSJS)** to provide a common national platform for recording and maintaining judicial statistics from across the country.

NSJS should provide real time statistics on cases and courts that will enable systematic analysis of key factors such as quality, timeliness and efficiency of the judicial system across courts, districts/states, types of cases, stages of cases, costs of adjudication, time lines of cases, productivity and efficiency of courts, use of budgets and financial resources. It would enhance transparency and accountability.

5. A **Court Development Planning System** that will provide a framework for systematic five year plans for the future development of the Indian judiciary. The planning system will include individual court development plans for all the courts.

6. A **Human Resource Development Strategy** setting standards on selection & training of judges of subordinate courts.

Out of the six main elements, the NSJS has been accomplished by starting the National Judicial Data Grid wherein every report pertaining to any Court throughout the country is made available online.

Thus it can be seen that reasons for delay in Civil Suits are endless. A Glance through the figures of cases filed in the courts over a number of years would clearly show that litigation has been increasing phenomenally in the Country and the Courts are over flooded with the cases. Procedure is the handmaid of justice. More and more Courts are required to be set up to keep pace with the increased number of cases. There is general feeling that the Government is *not appointing a sufficient number of Judges* to deal with the increasing work. Even existing vacancies in various High Courts remain unfilled for an unduly long time. Prompt appointment of Judges to fill the existing vacancies and creation of additional posts in sufficient number would go a long way to solve the problem of delay and arrears. Much of the delay occurs because *the provisions of the Code of Cicvil Procedure are not properly observed and followed*. The Judges have to be tailormade to cut short the average life of a civil suit. Today the Government is probably the biggest litigant in the Country. The _*inefficiency of the Governmental machinery*_ has also been responsible for considerable delay in disposal of cases where the Government is a party. The Judiciary is often criticized, in and out of Parliament, for mounting arrears of cases. What is forgotten, however, is the fact that the Government itself is responsible for the major portion of delay. The Judiciary is not in a position to give a public reply to the criticism leveled against it. *The attitude of some lawyers* is also to some extent responsible for delay as they keep applying for frequent adjournments on flimsy grounds. If lawyers are able to prolong the litigation by resorting to one or another, the question naturally arises, *why do judges allow lawyers to take advantage of procedural technalicalities and prolong litigation*? The Judges have to be tailormade to promptly decide such applications and thereby cutting short the average life of a civil suit. The judges must adopt 'No delay on my part' formula. Remember-*"Difficult roads often ends up with beautiful destinations."*

Chapter 5
Judicial Precedents and Guidelines

Law both substantive and adjective is product of human experiences gathered in its collective functioning at societal and institutional level. Legal methods and procedures are no exception and are product of time and they need fine tuning with change in circumstances based on experiences of its actual working. An honest search for reform is to be based on past experiences and cannot be tied to the rigidity of ideological moorings.

Justice Benjamin N. Cardozo in his book The Growth of The Law says, "We must learn that all methods are to viewed not as idols but as tools. We must test one of them by the others, supplementing and re-enforcing where there is weakness, so that what is strong and best in each will be at our service in the hour need". According to the famous quote of Oliver Wendell Holmes, Jr., 'the Life of the law has not been logic. It has been experience.[47]

---

[47] Judicial Academy Jharkhand, A Study on 'MAJOR BOTTLENECKS IN PROCEDURAL LAWS AFFECTING EXPEDITIOUS CONCLUSION OF CRIMINAL TRIALS AND MEASURES NEEDED TO REMOVE SUCH BOTTLENECKS', P.26.

The same analogy will apply with equal force to the vires of procedural law and any such Code which lays down procedures to further the ends of speedy justice without compromising the fair trial principles which do not prejudice the accused, can be regarded as just, fair and reasonable which is a constitutional requirement of any procedure under Article 21 of the Constitution of India post Maneka Gandhi verdict [48]. The Apex Court in **William Slaney vs. State of M.P**[49] held that the Criminal Procedure Code is a Code of procedure, and like all procedural laws, is designed to further the ends of justice and not to frustrate them by endless technicalities. The object of the code is to ensure that an accused person gets a full and fair trial along certain well established and well – understood lines that accord with our notions of natural justice. If it does, if it is tried by a competent court, if he is told certainly and clearly understands the nature of the offence for which he is being tried, if the case against him is fully / fairly explained to him and he is afforded a full and fair opportunity, of defending himself, then, provided there is substantial compliance with outward forms of the law, mere mistakes in procedures, mere

---

[48] (AIR 1978 SC 597).

[49] [1956] AIR (SC) 116.

inconsequential errors and omissions in the trial are regarded as venal the code and the trial is not vitiated unless the accused can show substantial prejudice.

Hon'ble Supreme Court of India in **Central Electricity Regulatory Commission Vs National Hydroelectric Power Corpn. Ltd. & Ors.**[50], has directed that in commercial litigation and in those cases where the Advocates seek urgent interim reliefs, service of notices may be effected by E-mail, in addition to normal mode of service. The apex court observed that in various courts, the statistical data indicates that, on account of delay in process serving, arrears keep on mounting. In Delhi itself, the input indicates that fifty percent of the arrears in courts particularly in commercial cases is on account of delay in process serving. The court further directed the Cabinet Secretariat to provide central e-mail addresses of various Ministries/Departments/Regulatory Authorities along with the names of the nodal officers appointed for the purposes of service.

---

[50] Civil Appeal No. 2010(D.21216/2010).

It has been further held by the Supreme Court in **Sunil Poddar vs Union Bank of India**[51] that if, the court is convinced that the defendant had otherwise knowledge of the proceedings and he could have appeared and answered the plaintiff's claim, he cannot put forward a ground of non-service of summons for setting aside ex-parte order passed against him by invoking Order IX Rule XIII of the Code.

In **Ravi Datt vs Chuni Lal**[52], the court observed that there are a large number of cases in which it is alleged that service has not been properly effected resulting in an ex parte decision followed by an application under Order IX Rule 13 of the CPC for setting aside the ex parte decision. This frequently happens not only in civil matters but also in matters arising under the Industrial Disputes Act, 1947. It is generally accepted that the process serving agency in the district courts needs an overhaul, to avoid recurrence of cases such as the present, and also to avoid a large number of applications being filed under Order IX Rule 13 of the CPC.

---

[51] Civil Appeal No. 86 of 2008.

[52] 2004 (75) DRJ 39.

In **Salem Advocates Bar Association, T.N v Union of India[53]**, It was observed that problem in respect of service of summons has been one of the major causes of delay in the due progress of the case. It is common knowledge that the defendants have been avoiding to accept summons. There have been serious problems in process serving agencies in various courts. There can, thus, be no valid objection in giving opportunity to the plaintiff to serve the summons on the defendant or get it served through courier. There is, however, danger of false reports of service. It is required to be adequately guarded. The courts shall have to be very careful while dealing with a case where orders for deemed service are required to be made on the basis of endorsement of such service or refusal. The high courts can make appropriate rules and regulations or issue practice directions to ensure that such provisions of service are not abused so as to obtain false endorsements. In this regard, the high courts can consider making a provision for filing of affidavit setting out details of events at the time of refusal of service. For instance, it can be provided that the affidavit of person effecting service shall state as to who all were present at that

---

[53] (2005) 6 SCC 344.

time and also that the affidavit shall be in the language known to the deponent. It can also be provided that if affidavit or any endorsement as to service is found to be false, the deponent can be summarily tried and punished for perjury and the courier company can be black-listed.

The apex court in **Zahira Habibullah Sheikh Vs. State of Gujarat**[54] observed that a criminal trial is a judicial examination of the issues in the case and its purpose is to arrive at a judgment on an issue as to a fact of relevant facts which may lead to the discovery of the fact in issue and obtain proof of such facts at which the prosecution and the accused have arrived by their pleadings; the controlling question being the guilt or innocence of the accused. Since the object is to meet out justice and to convict the guilty and protect the innocent, the trial should be a search for the truth and not a bout over technicalities and must be conducted under such rules as will protect the innocent and punish the guilty.

---

[54] (2006) 3 SCC 374.

In **AG Vs Shiv Kumar Yadav**[55] the Apex Court observed: "It can hardly be gainsaid that fair trial is a part of guarantee under Article 21 of the Constitution of India. Its content has primarily to be determined by the statutory provision for conduct of trial though in some matters, where statutory provision may be silent, the court may evolve a principle of law to meet a situation, which has not been provided for. It is also true that the principle of fair trial has to be kept in mind for interpreting the statutory provisions. It is further well settled that fairness of trial has to be seen not only from the point of view of the accused, but also from the point of view of the victim and the society."

Thus, it is a clear judicial trend that any procedure to be efficient and effective has not only to answer the test of logic and principles but also the experience of its actual working in the crucible of investigation, inquiry and trials'.

---

[55] [2015] 4 Crimes (SC) 1

Chapter 6
Role of a Judge

"Sometimes the judges of the higher courts think-and i am bound to say I thought sometimes myself- that the restoration of law and order depended upon what the high court judges did in dealing with the heavier cases. But i have finally come to the conclusion........that the real basis of establishment of law lies in the competency, honesty and fidelity of the lowest rank of judges."

-*Mr. Justice Hanna* (Irish Free Estate)

If an evaluation is made of the importance of the role of the different functionaries who play their part in the administration of justice, the top position would necessarily have to be assigned to the trial court judge. India has one of the largest judicial systems in the world with over 3 crore cases and sanctioned strength of some 18,871 Judges. Hence, the trial court judge is the key-man and the most important and influential participant in our judicial system. The common man really forms an impression about the judiciary from the working of the trial courts.

This is because he is concerned with the Judges and the courts at the bottom only. His hopes are pinned with the subordinate judiciary. The image of the judiciary for the common man, therefore, is projected by the trial court Judges and this. In turn, depends upon their intellectual, moral and personal qualities. Therefore, in the arduous task of disposal of old unyielding and time-consuming cases, the great qualities of head and heart of the trial court Judge and the influence of his personality go a long way.

Hon'ble Supreme Court in its landmark judgment of All India Judges Association v. Union of India[56], has observed that the trial Judge is the king pin in the hierarchical system of administration of justice. He directly comes in contact with the litigant during the proceedings in Court. On him lies the responsibility of building up of the case appropriately and on his understanding of the matter the cause of justice is first answered. The personality knowledge, judicial restraint, capacity to maintain dignity are the additional aspects which go into making the Court's functioning successful."

---

[56] AIR 1992 SC 165.

Judiciary in India enjoys a very significant position since it has been made the guardian and custodian of the Constitution. It not only is a watchdog against violation of fundamental rights guaranteed under the Constitution and thus insulates all persons, Indians and aliens alike, against discrimination, abuse of State power, arbitrariness etc. but borrowing the words of one of the founding fathers of the American Constitution, James Medison, I would say that the Judiciary in India is "truly the only defensive armour of the country and its constitution and laws". If this armour were to be stripped of its onerous functions it would mean, "the door is wide open for nullification, anarchy and convulsion". Liberty and Equality have well survived and thrived in India due to the pro-active role played by the Indian judiciary. The rule of law, one of the most significant characteristics of good governance prevails because India has an independent judiciary that has been sustained, amongst others, because of support and assistance from an independent bar which has been fearless in advocating the cause of the underprivileged, the cause of deprived, the cause of such sections of society as are ignorant or unable to secure their rights owing to various handicaps, an enlightened public opinion and vibrant media that keeps all the agencies of the State on their respective toes.

Thus, it can be seen that subordinate Judiciary is the backbone of Indian Judiciary. It is the base on which the judicial edifice of the country rests. The base must, therefore, be sufficiently strong to carry the weight of the Judicial system. The Image of the judicial system in the public eye rests on the members of the subordinate Judiciary since it is they who come in direct contact with the litigant public. Therefore, a heavy duty and responsibility lies on them to function in a manner as would enhance the image of the judiciary and Its credibility in the public eye.[57]

---

[57]Mr. Justice A. M. Ahmadi, former Chief Justice of India in his lecture on the subordinate courts.

Chapter 7

ADR and Mediation

Alternative dispute resolution (ADR) is a dispute resolution technique used to resolve disagreements and disputes between parties by coming to an agreeable settlement through discussion and negotiation. Conciliation and arbitration are two such forms of ADR that are used as an alternative to going to courts to resolve conflicts.

By the CPC (amendment) Act 1999, section 89 had been introduced in the CPC, 1908 and it became effective from 01-07-2002. Section 89 in CPC reads as follows;

"Section 89. Settlement of disputes outside the Court- (1) Where it appears to the court that there exist elements of a settlement which may be acceptable to the parties, the court shall formulate the terms of settlement and give them to the parties for their observations and after receiving the observation of the parties, the court may reformulate the terms of a possible settlement and refer the same for- (a) arbitration;(b) conciliation(c) judicial settlement including settlement through Lok Adalat; or (d) mediation.

(2) Where a dispute had been referred-

(a) for arbitration or conciliation, the provisions of the Arbitration and Conciliation Act, 1996 shall apply as if the proceedings for arbitration or conciliation were referred for settlement under the provisions of that Act.

(b) to Lok Adalat, the court shall refer the same to the Lok Adalat in accordance with the provisions of sub-section (1) of section 20 of the Legal Services Authority Act, 1987 and all other provisions of that Act shall apply in respect of the dispute so referred to the Lok Adalat;

(c) for judicial settlement, the court shall refer the same to a suitable institution or person and such institution or person shall be deemed to be a Lok Adalat and all the provisions of the Legal Services Authority Act, 1987 shall apply as if the dispute were referred to a Lok Adalat under the provisions of that Act;

(d) for mediation, the court shall effect a compromise between the parties and shall follow such procedure as may be prescribed.

The related provisions which were incorporated by the same amendment act are those contained in Rules 1A, 1B and 1C of Order X, CPC.

Thus, it can be seen that Section 89 starts with the words **"where it appears to the court that there exist elements of a settlement"**. This clearly shows that cases which are not suited for ADR process should not be referred under section 89 of the Code.

The court has to form an opinion that a case is one that is capable of being referred to and settled through ADR process. Having regard to the tenor of the provisions of Rule 1A of Order 10 of the Code, the civil court should invariably refer cases to ADR process. Only in certain recognized excluded categories of cases, it may choose not to refer to an ADR process.

Where the case is unsuited for reference to any of the ADR process, the court will have to briefly record the reasons for not resorting to any of the settlement procedures prescribed under section 89 of the Code. Therefore, having a hearing after completion of pleadings, to consider recourse to ADR process under section 89 of the Code, is mandatory.

The initiatives taken by the Supreme Court in **Salem Advocate Bar Association v. Union of India**[58] and **Salem Advocate Bar Association v. Union of India (II)**[59], gave the initial momentum to use of ADR in courts pursuant to section 89 CPC.

---

[58]AIR 2003 SC 189.
[59]AIR 2005 SC 3353.

If for any reason, the court did not refer the case to ADR process before framing issues, nothing prevents the court from considering reference even at a later stage. In the case of Apex Court in **Salem Bar Association (III)** (Supra) , Section 89 proceeding at appellate stage:-There is no dispute to the settled legal provision that the pleading can be amendment at any stage .A party can also be impleaded at any stage the proceeding. In such an eventuality ,as the appeal is a continuation of suit, there should be no problem in resorting to the procedure prescribed under Section 89 by the Court at appellate stage. Having regard to the provisions of Section 89 and Rule 1-A of Order 10, the stage at which the court should explore whether the matter should be referred to ADR processes, is after the pleadings are complete, and before framing the issues, when the matter is taken up for preliminary hearing for examination of parties under Order 10 of the Code.

However, if for any reason, the court had missed the opportunity to consider and refer the matter to ADR processes under Section 89 before framing issues, nothing prevents the court from resorting to Section 89 even after framing issues. But once evidence is commenced, the court will be reluctant to refer the matter to the ADR processes lest it becomes a tool for protracting the Trial.

Section 89 of CPC vests the choice of reference to the court. There is of course no inconsistency, section 89 of the code gives the jurisdiction to refer to ADR Process and Rules 1 A to !C o order 10 lay down the manner in which the said jurisdiction is to be exercised. the scheme is the court explains the available regarding ADR process to the parties them to opt for a process by consensus and if there is no consensus proceed to choose the process. The referral judge plays a crucial role even after the conclusion of mediation. Even though the dispute was referred for mediation the court retains its control and jurisdiction over the matter If there is no settlement between the parties, the court proceedings shall continue in accordance with law.[60]

---

[60] Afcons Infrastructure Ltd. Vs. Cherian Varkey Construction Co. (P) Ltd., reported in AIR 2010 SCW 4983.

- **Conciliation and Arbitration**

    The conciliation process is handled by an impartial individual known as a conciliator, who meets with the parties involved and works with the parties involved to arrive at a settlement or resolution. Whereas, Arbitration is much like a mini court in which the parties need to present their case to a panel of arbitrators, along with supporting evidence.

    Conciliation and arbitration are two such forms of ADR that are used as an alternative to going to courts to resolve conflicts.

- **Judicial Settlement**

    In Judicial Settlement the concerned Judge tries to settle the dispute between the parties amicably. Such settlement will be deemed to be decree within the meaning of the Legal Services Authorities Act, 1987. Section 89 C of C.P.C. Provides for judicial settlement that the Court shall refer the same to a suitable institution or person and such institution or person shall be deemed to be a Lok Adalat and all the provisions of the Legal Services Authority Act, 1987 (39 of 1987) shall apply as if the dispute were referred to a Lok Adalat under the provisions of that Act.

However, there are no specified rules framed so far for such settlement. It has been provided therein that when there is a Judicial Settlement the provisions of the Legal Services Authorities Act, 1987 CPC 89 will apply. There are no written guidelines prescribed in India as to judicial settlement.

- **Lok Adalat**

Section 89 B of the C.P.C. Provides for Lok Adalat that the Court shall refer the case to the Lok Adalat in accordance with provisions of the Legal Services Authority Act, 1987.

When the matter is referred to the Lok Adalat then the provisions of the Legal Services Authorities Act, 1987 will apply. But it has been provided therein that when there is a Judicial Settlement the provisions of the Legal Services Authorities Act, 1987 & CPC will apply Lok adalat award is deemed to be decree within the meaning of the Legal Services Authorities Act, 1987. no appeal lies against this order.

But actual reference to an ADR process in all cases is not mandatory. Where the case falls under an excluded category there need not be reference ton ADR process. In all other case reference to ADR process is a must.

- **Mediation**

Mediation can be done simultaneously with exploring possibilities of a legal action on the civil or the criminal jurisdiction. It is a voluntary process and most people are attracted to the option of mediation because-

1. it promotes the interest of the entire family including those of the children; and
2. it reduces economic and emotional cost associated with the resolution of the family disputes.

As approved in the meeting of the hon'ble mediation monitoring committee held on 5.8.2011 and implemented in the state of Gujarat w.e.f. 15.8.2011 and In case of Hon'ble Supreme Court of India **K. Srinivas Rao vs D.A. Deepa** on 22 February, 2013,.jjudgment para 3. The idea of per-litigation mediation is also catching up.

Some mediation centres have, after giving wide publicity, set up "Help Desks" at prominent places including facilitation centres at court complexes to conduct per-litigation mediation.

- **Mediation Processs**

The mediation process is initiated through a referral order. The referral judge should understand the importance of a referral order in the mediation process and should not have a casual approach in passing the order. The referral order is the foundation of a court-referred mediation. An ideal referral order should contain among other things details like name of the referral judge, case number, name of the parties, date and year of institution of the case, stage of trial, nature of the dispute, the statutory provision under which the reference is made, next date of hearing before the referral court, whether the parties have consented for mediation, name of the institution/mediator to whom the case is referred for mediation, the date and time for the parties to report before the institution/ mediator, the time limit for completing the mediation, quantum of fee/remuneration if payable and contact address and telephone numbers of the parties and their advocates. Referral Judge should make an objective assessment whether the case is fit for mediation. Section 89 read with Order 10, 1(A), 1(B) and 1(C) of the Code of Civil Procedure is the source of power of a Referral Judge.

Before referring a case, a Referral Judge should have knowledge of the relevant facts and should satisfy himself that the case involves an element of settlement by way of mediation. A good Referral Judge has to identify categories of cases which are suitable for mediation.

Referral Judge can send a case for mediation even without the consent of the parties if he finds that there is an element of settlement. But all the same, he must be conscious of the fact or he must guide himself that mediation shall not be a devise to delay the proceedings. Further, it may be relevant to note that certain disputes may not be appropriate for mediation including the cases involving criminal offense which involve novel question of law, dispute where one party strives for legal precedent, or the dispute which affects the large number of persons or the society in general, etc.

AS per Rule 2 (4) The mediation shall not be limited only to the issues in the refereed dispute and the mediator may take into account the dispute between the parties to a case which are not the subject of the pending litigation, and may resolve all dispute between the parties.

Rule 18 of the Mediation Rule prescribes time limit for completing of mediation on expiry of ninety days from the date fixed for the first appearance of the parties before the mediator the mediation shall stand terminated, unless the court which referred the matter either suo moto or upon request by any of the parties and upon hearing all the parties, is of the view that extension of time is necessary or may be useful but such extension shall not be beyond a further period of thirty days.

On settlement of dispute between the parties, same shall be recorded in writing with the signature of the parties concerned and mediator, Such settlement shall be referred to the Lok adalat or PLA concerned Court. Such Lok adalat shall record the same as an agreement between the parties and shall pass appropriate award contemplated under section 21 of the Legal services authority act 1987. Original award shall be kept with the concerned Legal Service Authority and one copy thereof free of cost shall be supplied to the parties concerned in the first instance.

- **Judicial Guidelines**

As per the judgment of **M.P. State Legal Service ... vs Prateek Jain And Anr** on 10 September, 2014 it was observed that having regard thereto, we are of the opinion that even when a case is decided in Lok Adalat, the requirement of following the guidelines contained in Damodar S. Prabhu (supra) should normally not be dispensed with. However, if there is a special/specific reason to deviate therefrom, the Court is not remediless as Damodar S. Prabhu (supra) itself has given discretion to the concerned Court to reduce the costs with regard to specific facts and circumstances of the case, while recording reasons in writing about such variance. Therefore, in those matters where the case has to be decided/settled in the Lok Adalat, **if the Court finds that it is a result of positive attitude of the parties, in such appropriate cases, the Court can always reduce the costs by imposing minimal costs or even waive the same.** For that, it would be for the parties, particularly the accused person, to make out a plausible case for the waiver/reduction of costs and to convince the concerned Court about the same.

This course of action, according to us, would strike a balance between the two competing but equally important interests, namely, achieving the objectives delineated in Damodar S. Prabhu (supra) on the one hand and the public interest which is sought to be achieved by encouraging settlements/resolution of case through Lok Adalats.

Thereafter in **Afcons Infrastructure Ltd. v. Cherian Varkey Construction Co. (P) Ltd.**[61], which can be described as a comprehensive practical guide for effective use of section 89 CPC, the Supreme Court has given detailed practical guidelines so that section 89 CPC can be utilized so as to achieve the best results. In Afcons Infrastructure Ltd. the Supreme Court has also directed interchange of clauses (c) and (d) of section 89 (2) CPC by interpretative process to correct the draftsman's error so that section 89 CPC is not rendered meaningless and infructuous.

---

[61]JT 2010 (7) SC 616.

BIBLIOGRAPHY

A. List of Cases

- A. C. Narayanan v. State of Maharashtra, AIR 2014 SUPREME COURT 630.

- Arjuna Lai Dhanji Rathod v. Dayaram Premji Padhiar, AIR 1971 Pat. 278

- ASHOK YESHWANT BADEVE V. SURENDRA MADHAVRAO NIGHOJAKARAIR 2001 SUPREME COURT 1315.

- Aparna A. Shah v. M/s. Sheth Developers Pvt. Ltd., AIR 2013 SUPREME COURT 3210.

- Anwar Ali Prop. Samira Export, Mumbai v. State of U.P. 2004(50) JLC; 2004(2) 659.

- Assoo Hajee vs. K.I. Abdul Latheef 2005 Cr. L. J. 640 (Ker)

- Baker v. Australia and New Zealand Bank Ltd(1958) NZLR 907
- Capital and Counties Bank v. Gordon, (1903) AC 240
- Cucusan Foils Private Co. Ltd. v. State (Delhi Administration), 1990(2) Recent Criminal Reports,518
- Dashrath Rupsingh Rathod vs. State of Mah. and Anr2014 (9) SCC 129
- Electronics Trade & Technology Development Corpn Ltd. v. Indian Technologists & Engineers Electronics Pvt. Ltd.

- Flach v. London & South Western Bank Ltd. (1915) 31 TLR334
- G.F. Hunasi Katti Math v. State of Karnataka, I (1991) BC 438: 1991 (1) Crimes 227
- HARBANS SINGH v. SUNDDER MAL SAT PAL, I (2000) BC 472 (P&H).
- ICDS Ltd. Vs. Beena Shabeer &Anr. (2002) 6 SCC 426
- INDIAN BANK ASSOCIATION AND OTHERS V. UNION OF INDIA, (2014) 5 SCC 590
- JAGDISH SINGH VS. NATTHU SINGH; STATE OF M.P. VS. HIRALAL AND ORS.
- KAMLESH KUMAR VS. STATE OF BIHAR & ANR, CRIMINAL APPEAL NO. 2083/2013, S.C., ON DE. 11, 2013.
- K.K.C. Textiles Mills v. Maize Products (1998) 3 Crimes 509 (Mad.)
- London Joint Stock Bank v. Macmillan & Arthur,(1918) AC 777.
- Mahalakshmi Enterprises v. Shri Visnu Trading & Co. AIR 1991 Andh. P.74.
- Mayri Pulse Mills v. Union of India, (1996) 86 Comp Cas 121 Bom.
- M/S. Goyal Mg Gases Pvt.Ltd. vs State & Ors [2015 (1) DCR 169]
- MSR LEATHERS VS. S.PALANIAPPAN AND ANOTHER.(2013) 1 SCC 177.

- MICHAEL KURUVILLA V. JOSEPH J. KONDODY, 1998(3) CRIMES 54 (KER.)

- MEHSANAN NAGRIK SAHKARI BANK LTD. V. SHREEJI CAB CO. A ND OTHERS, S.C., DT.12 JULY 2013.

- MANJU M. AGARWAL V. COUNSEL FOR DECIDED ON 26 MARCH, 2014 BY ANDRA H.C.

- M.M.MALIK V. PREM KUMAR GOYAL, II (1991) BC 484: 1991 CRI L.J. 2594
- NATIONAL SMALL INDUSTRIES CORPORATION LTD. V. STATE (NCT OF DELHI).AIR 2009 SUPREME COURT 1284.
- NITINBHAI SEVANTILAL SHAH V. MANUBHAI MANJIBHAI PANCHAL, AIR 2011 SC 307.
- NIRMAL SINGH KAHLON V. STATE OF PUNJAB & ORS. ; AIR 2008 SC 441.

- State (NCT of Delhi) v. Navjot Sandhu alias Afsan Guru, (2005) 11 SCC 600

- NARAYANADAS BHAGWANDAS PARTANI V. UNION OF INDIA, 1993 MAH LJ 1229
- OM PARKASH BHOJRAJ MANIYAR V. SWATI GIRISH BHIDE, 1992 MAH L.J. 302: 1992(3) CRIMES 306
- PUNJAB AND SIND BANK V. VINKAR SAHAKARI BANK LTD. 2001(7)SCC 721.

- Plunkett v. Barclays Bank Ltd, (1936) 2 KB 107: (1936) 1 All ER 653: 154 LT 465.
- Patel Dineshkumar Shivram Somdas v. Patel Keshavlal Mohanlal 2000 Cr.L.J. 3547 (Guj.)

- Payare Lal V/s. State of Punjab, AIR 1962 SC 690.

- Prof. Veda Vyasa v. Satija Builders & Financiers Ltd., II (1992) BC 146
- Rakesh Nemkumar Porwal v. Narayan Dhondu Joglekar, 1993 Cri L.J. 680: II (1992) BC 402: 1992 CCR 2711: 1993(78) Comp. Cas 822.
- Rahul Builders v/s Arihant Fertilizers & Chemicals, 2008 Cr.L.J. 452 SC
- Ravi Chopra v. State &Anr., 2008 (102) DRJ 147.
- Sant Priya Engineers (Pvt.) Ltd. v. Uday Sankar Das (1998) 91 Comp. Cas. 599 (Cal.)

- Saket India Ltd. v. India Securities Ltd. AIR 1999 SC 1090.
- Sandeep Khanna & Anr. v. State & Ors., MANU/DE/2364/2010.
- Suresh Chandra Goyal vs Amit Singhal, Delhi High Court, 14 May, 2015.
- Sangeetaben Mahendrabhai Patel vs. State of Gujarat and Anr, MANU/SC/0321/2012.
- Sai Auto Agencies through its partner Dnyandeo Ramdas Rane v. Sheikh Yusuf Sheikh Umar, 2011 (1) Crimes 180.
- Syed Rasool & Sons v. Aildas & Co., 1992 Cri L.J. 4048: 1993(11) Crimes 550: (1993) 78 Comp Cas. 738
- Sukanraja Khimraja, a firm of Merchants, Bombay v. N. Rajagopalan, 1989 1 LW 401
- Thomas Varghese v. P. Jerome, 1992 Cri L.J. 308

- Tripti Vyas v. State of Rajsthan; IV(2013) BC 335 (Raj.)

- Underwood Ltd. v. Barclays Banks, (1924) 1 KB 775
- Union Roadways v. Shah Raman Lai Satish Kumar, II (1992) BC 216: 76 Comp Cas (AP) 3151.
- V.S. Krishnan v. V.S. Narayanan, 1990(1) MWN (Cri) Mad 75: 1990 LW (Cri) 66
- V.S. Krishnan v. Narayana, 1990 (1) MWN (Cr) Mad 75:1990 LW (Cr) 66.
- VISHNU SPINNERS V. SHRI BHAGYALAKSHMI COMMERCIAL CORP. 1999 CR.L.J. 1221 (A.P.)

B. List of Books, Journals and Periodicals, Websites

- Azad S.A.K., Indian Judiciary: A Saviour of Life and Personal Liberty, A.I.R. 2000 (Journal Section) 17.
- Bhagwati P.N., Enforcement of Fundamental Rights: Role of Courts, Paper presented at Judicial Colloquium in Bangalore, February, 1988.
- Bad Check Laws by States, **http://www.ckfraud.org/**.
- Bills of Exchange Act, 1882, **http://www.legislation.gov.uk/**.
- Cheque Bounce offence likely to go, http://articles.economictimes.indiatimes.com/ .

- Dhananjay Mahapatra, Recovering Cheque Bounce to get more tedious, **http://timesofindia.indiatimes.com/**.
- Double Jeopardy in India, http://www.legalservicesindia.com/.
- Enforcing Contracts, http://www.doingbusiness.org/.
- Legal era, Section 138 of Negotiable Instruments Act, 1881- the law, leading judgements of 2012 and the lacunae, http://www.legalera.in/.
- Payment of Cheques in France, http://www.french-property.com/.
- Sandeep Jalan, Literally, S. 138 was enacted for no reason, http://commonlaw-sandeep.blogspot.in/.
- Section 76, Cheques Act 1986, http://www5.austlii.edu.au/.
- Shubho Roy, The Saga of Criminalising and then Decriminalising Cheque Bouncing, http://ajayshahblog.blogspot.in/.
- Raj Kachroo, Report of the First Phase of Work Done On Judicial Reform, March 2012.
- Machinery in India, the Academy Law Review, Volume XXIII (1999).
- Gupta J.P., Emerging Socio-Economic Trends: Role of Lawyers and Legal Institutions, A.I.R. 1999 (Journal Section) 175.

C. List of Abbreviations and ACRONYMS
- ADR : Alternative Dispute Resolution
- AIR : All India Reports
- CESCR : Committee on Economic, Social and Cultural Rights

- CJ : Chief Justice
- CrPC : Criminal Procedure Code
- ECOWAS : Economic Community of Western African States
- ECOWAS : Economic Community of West African States
- FR : Fundamental Right(s)
- HC : High Court
- ICCR : International Covenant on Civil and Political Rights
- ICESC : International Covenant on Economic, Social & Cultural
- IO : Investigating Officer
- IPC : Indian Penal Code
- NI : Negotiable Instrument
- RTI : Right to Information Act, 2005
- SC : Scheduled Caste/Supreme Court
- SCC : Supreme Court Cases
- SCR : Supreme Court Reports
- ST : Scheduled Tribes
- UN : United Nations
- UNDP : United Nations Development Programme
- UPR : Universal Periodic Review
- WG : Working Group

****